CONTENTS

Skateboarding words are explained on pages 30 and 31.

I AM A SKATEBOARDING FREAK

James Kitchen Factfile
Age: Fifteen
Years skating: Fourteen months
Favourite pros: Eric Koston, Paul Rodriguez and Tony Trujillo.
Hobbies: Skateboarding, filming skateboarding and skateboarding.

Me at my local skate spot, where it all began.

I'm James Kitchen, but my friends call me 'Kitch' – shouting 'Kitchen!' across the skatepark sounds pretty strange. This is the story of how I got into skateboarding. The story comes from the diary I've kept ever since I first stepped on a skateboard. I made notes of all the most important moments of my skating life. My first ollie, my first day at a proper skatepark ... even my first slam! Maybe one day when I become a famous pro skater this diary will be worth a fortune. But then again, maybe it won't ...

Tony Trujillo draws the crowd's attention.

Diary of a SKATEBOARDING Freak

www.heinemann.co.uk/library
Visit our website to find out more information about **Heinemann Library** books.

To order:
 Phone 44 (0) 1865 888066
 Send a fax to 44 (0) 1865 314091
Visit the Heinemann Bookshop at www.heinemann.co.uk/library to browse our catalogue and order online.

Produced by Monkey Puzzle Media Ltd
Gissing's Farm, Fressingfield, Suffolk IP21 5SH, UK

First published in Great Britain by Heinemann Library, Halley Court, Jordan Hill, Oxford OX2 8EJ, part of Harcourt Education. Heinemann is a registered trademark of Harcourt Education Ltd.

This paperback edition published in 2005
© Monkey Puzzle Media Ltd 2004
The moral right of the proprietor has been asserted.

Author: Ben Powell
Editorial: Paul Mason
Series Design: Mayer Media Ltd
Book Design: Mayer Media Ltd
Illustrator: Sam Lloyd
Production: Séverine Ribierre

Originated by Repro Multi-Warna
Printed in China by WKT Company Limited

ISBN 0 431 17532 2 (hardback)
08 07 06 05
10 9 8 7 6 5 4 3 2

ISBN 0 431 17537 3 (paperback)
09 08 07 06 05
10 9 8 7 6 5 4 3 2 1

British Library Cataloguing in Publication Data
Powell, Ben
Diary of a Skateboarding Freak
796.2'2
A full catalogue record for this book is available from the British Library.

Acknowledgements
With thanks to **Will Linford** for supplying all photographs, with the exception of: **3 centre left, bottom left** and **top right, 13 both, 14 bottom, 16 both, 17, 27 bottom** supplied by **Leo Sharpe.**

Every effort has been made to contact copyright holders of any material reproduced in this book. Any omissions will be rectified in subsequent printings if notice is given to the publishers.

Attention!

This book is about skateboarding, which is a dangerous sport. This book is not an instruction manual or a substitute for proper lessons. Every year people are hurt riding skateboards – make sure you aren't one of them. Get expert instruction, always wear the right safety equipment, and make sure you ride within your own ability.

One day, stair jumps like this will be mine!

MAY

3	10	17	24	31
4	11	18	25	
5	12	19	26	
6	13	20	27	
7	14	21	28	
8	15	22	29	
1	9	16	23	30
2				

TRUCKS — MADE FROM STEEL WITH AN AXLE THAT IS USED TO GRIND OBJECTS. YOU CAN TIGHTEN OR LOOSEN THE TRUCKS BY ADJUSTING THE KINGPIN NUT.

DECK — MADE FROM THIN SHEETS OF MAPLE PLYWOOD GLUED TOGETHER, THEN SHAPED IN A MOULD. GRIP TAPE ON OTHER SIDE.

BEGINNER DAYS

Yesterday was my fourteenth birthday, and I got my first proper board from the skater-owned shop in town. My new board is so much faster and easier to control than the old one I had been using! I'm stoked on the feeling of just riding along on this new set up. My dad agreed to take me to the local skatepark, as long as I wore my helmet. He's worried that I'm going to hurt myself, but I've got more control than he thinks. All those days pushing around on the driveway have paid off!

WHEELS — MADE FROM POLYURETHANE. MY WHEELS ARE 56 MM IN DIAMETER WITH A 101A READING ON THE DUROMETER: THAT'S PRETTY HARD SO THESE WHEELS ARE REALLY FAST.

A 'KICK', AT THE FRONT (AND BACK) OF THE BOARD.

DROPPING IN

I was a little bit intimidated by all the other skaters at first, so I found a quiet corner and started learning to drop in on one of the smaller ramps. Eventually I worked it out and by the end of the day I could drop in every go.
It feels amazing.

New helmet and pads.

JUNE

	7	14	21	28
1	8	15	22	29
2	9	16	23	30
3	10	17	24	
4	11	18	25	
5	12	19	26	
6	13	20	27	

Pushing — I push with my back foot, with my front foot pointing towards the nose of my board. As I push off and begin to pick up speed I turn my front foot so that it's sideways and put my back foot back on.

BASICS

Since my first skatepark session I've been practising basic techniques every night. One of the guys in the skate shop explained to me that it was important to make sure that I learned all of the basics before I began trying tricks. He says that a lot of younger skaters ignore them, and they end up with 'stinking style'. He must know what he's talking about: he's a really good skater!

RAMP PUMPING TIPS:

• Pumping is the name that skaters give to the technique for keeping your speed on ramps.

• Keeping your knees bent lets you shift your weight around.

• You have to throw your body weight up the transition of the ramp and then back down it again.

JULY

```
      5   12  19  26
      6   13  20  27
      7   14  21  28
  1   8   15  22  29
  2   9   16  23  30
  3   10  17 (24) 31
  4   11  18  25
```

BREAKTHROUGH!

I finally learned how to ollie at the skatepark today! I was beginning to think that I'd never work it out and then all of a sudden I just did one. I've been meeting up with my friend Sam at the park every night after school. He's only been skating for a little while too, and it's much easier to learn with somebody else at the same level. We've both been watching an instructional video that explains the ollie step by step. It seems to be working!

PUT YOUR BACK FOOT ON THE TAIL WITH YOUR FRONT FOOT BEHIND THE FRONT TRUCK BOLTS. CROUCH AND POP THE TAIL AGAINST THE FLOOR AS HARD AS YOU CAN.

AS THE TAIL HITS THE GROUND, SUCK YOUR WEIGHT UPWARDS AND DRAG YOUR FRONT FOOT UP THE BOARD AND FORWARDS TO CONTROL THE OLLIE.

File	Status	Time	Transfer
✓ Skate info.sit	Complete	< 1 minute	1.7 MB

Download Manager

THE HISTORY OF THE OLLIE

Alan 'Ollie' Gelfand invented the ollie in Florida, back in the late 1970s.

The ollie is the basis of all other modern tricks.

Before the ollie skaters couldn't jump into the air without grabbing their boards.

England's Danny Wainwright holds the world record for the highest flatland ollie, with 113 cm off the flat!

LAND ON ALL FOUR WHEELS SIMULTANEOUSLY AND CROUCH TO ABSORB THE IMPACT.

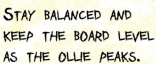

STAY BALANCED AND KEEP THE BOARD LEVEL AS THE OLLIE PEAKS.

It's easier to balance if you make sure that your feet are above the truck bolts at either end of the board.

Tricks like these in parks and on the streets would be impossible if the ollie hadn't been invented!

11

AUGUST

2	9	16	23	30
3	10	17	24	31
4	11	18	25	
5	12	19	26	
6	13	20	27	
7	14	21	28	
1 8	15	22	29	

BARCELONA DREAMING

Got an email today from a Spanish skater my sister has met at university in Barcelona. Javier told me all about a spot called MACBA, which sounds incredible! The floor is made from marble so it's really smooth and fast. All around the building there are flat banks, blocks and stairs to skate.

Skating contests apparently draw massive crowds in Barcelona.

Inbox	Compose
Reply	Reply All

From: Javier Montoya
To: James Kitchen
Subject: MACBA
Date: 1/8

Hola James! Your sister tells me that you are really into skateboarding. You should come to Barcelona to visit, my friend; I would show you the many spots that are here in Barcelona. You will probably recognize most of them from skate videos and magazines. The weather is great and you are allowed to skate at places like MACBA because the artists who work there really like skateboarding. I've attached a few photographs of the place for you to look at.

Barcelona is full of the weirdest skateboard obstacles, their approach to skateparks is unique. Look at the size of the bank that Pete Rigby is ollieing into! He must have been going so fast when he rode away from this one...

People travel from all over the world to skate in Barcelona. The surfaces are smooth, the weather is beautiful, skateboarding lives and breathes there. Here Ben Blake from Australia nosegrinds one of the blocks at MACBA, to a 180 out.

13

SEPTEMBER

6	13	20	27
7	14	21	28
1	8	15	22	29
2	9	16	23	30
3	10	17	24
4	11	18	25
5	12	19	26

TECHNICAL TRICKS

Sam and I have got hold of another instructional video, which has all of the more technical tricks explained on it. We're both trying to learn kickflips at the moment, but it's really hard to get your front foot back on the board while it's flipping in the air. We managed to take photos of one attempt that worked, but most still seem to be ending in failure!

Matt Harfield: kickflip over barrier.

14

Freestyle skater Rodney Mullen invented the kickflip back in the early 1980s. Rodney also invented most of the other flip tricks, including the heelflip, 360 flip and hardflip.

Variations I want to learn:
● Varial flip
● Frontside and backside flips
● 360 flips

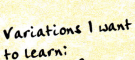

4	11	18	25
5	12	19	26
6	13	20	27
7	14	21	28
1	8	15	22	29
2	9	16	23	30
3	10	(17)	24	31

Shell Centre — this is one of the most famous sets of stairs in the UK. I ollied them today! The run-up is really smooth and the area is apparently always deserted. Daniel Kinloch skates the Shell stairs all the time: this is a beast of a nollie kickflip.

TRIP TO THE CITY

Just back from a visit to my aunt and uncle in London. I persuaded dad to stop off at a few of London's most famous skate spots on the way back. He wasn't too keen about me skating around a big city on my own, so he watched while I skated the stairs. This was the first time that my dad's actually seen me skate for quite a while. He seemed really impressed with how much better I've got.

Playstation — London's biggest indoor skatepark. Indoor parks are really important in the UK because it rains so much. The wooden surface isn't as fast as a concrete one but it's much softer to fall on! Wooden parks tend to have more obstacles, so I think that they're better for a beginner like me.

Meanwhile 2 —
This is an old concrete park that was built in the 1970s during the first craze of skateboarding. Modern skateparks are completely different from this mellow dish bowl with a gap. Skaters still come here a lot because it's so unique.

NOVEMBER

1	8	15	22	29
2	9	16	23	30
3	10	17	24	
4	11	18	25	
5	12	19	26	
6	13	20	27	
7	14	21	28	

CONCRETE SKATING

I've just found out that we're going to Edinburgh for the weekend. My friend Sam is coming. Dad has promised to take us to Livingston skatepark for an afternoon while we're there! This is going to be amazing. I just hope it doesn't rain!

'Livi'

Livi was built in the early 1980s, at a time when skateboarding wasn't very popular and when very few skateparks were being built in concrete. Today it's one of the most famous skateparks in the world. Hundreds of skaters travel there to attend the annual 'Livi Pure Fun Skate Party', which has been running for over 20 years.

The sun even came out — the local skaters told us this doesn't happen all that often! This place was so massive, we didn't know what to skate first...

18

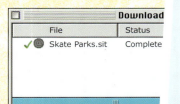

I liked the bowl best. It's so fast and big, really different from the feeling of street skating.

Concrete parks tend to have bigger and more challenging obstacles than wooden parks. Skate bowls are almost always made from concrete. Skateboarding as we know it today was invented in drained backyard swimming pools in the USA in the 1970s. Livi bowl follows the shape of a backyard pool but is much bigger.

All the obstacles in concrete skateparks like Livi are linked together, so you can skate much faster than normal. Skating more than one obstacle in a row is known as 'skating a line'.

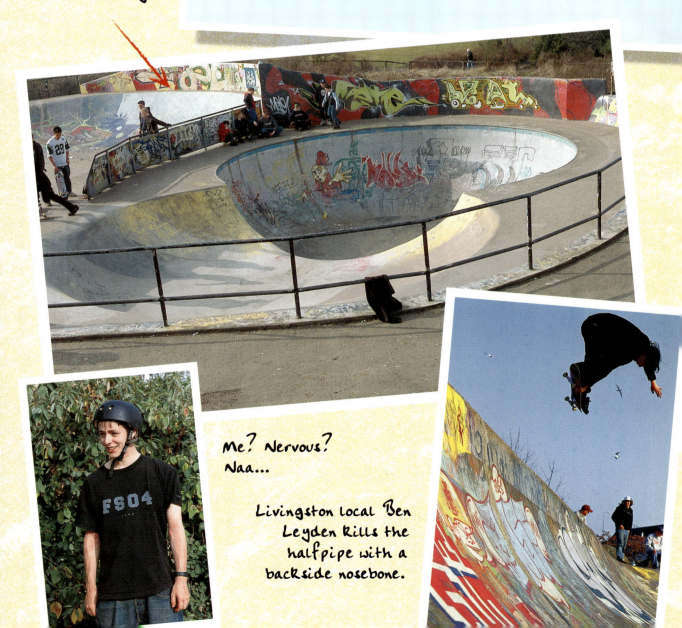

Me? Nervous? Naa...

Livingston local Ben Leyden kills the halfpipe with a backside nosebone.

APRIL

4	11	18	25
5	12	19	26
6	13	20	27
7	14	21	28
1	8	15	22	29
2	9	16	23	30
3	10	17	(24)	

ROCK AND ROLL!

TRANSITION SKATING

Sam and I need to work on our transition skating skills, so we've been down to the skatepark again. Skating transitions is skating on the curves of ramps or skatepark obstacles, rather than the flat ground of the street. On transitions you have to be comfortable doing tricks while going really fast, and I never skate that fast on the street. We've been to our local mini ramp and have been practising a few basic tricks.

2) AS YOUR FRONT WHEELS REACH THE LIP PUT WEIGHT ON YOUR BACK FOOT AND LET YOUR BOARD LAP OVER ON TO THE PLATFORM.

1) RIDE UP THE TRANSITION FORWARDS.

50–50! →

1) RIDE UP THE TRANSITION FORWARDS.

2) AT THE TOP, TURN YOURSELF THROUGH 90 DEGREES AND LEAN BACK ON TO THE PLATFORM.

20

3) PAUSE FOR A SECOND, THEN TURN YOUR SHOULDERS AND LEAN ON TO YOUR BACK FOOT AGAIN, TWISTING BACK INTO THE RAMP.

4) RIDE AWAY.

4) TURN BACK INTO THE RAMP AND RIDE AWAY.

3) GRIND ALONG THE COPING ON YOUR TRUCKS UNTIL YOU BEGIN TO SLOW DOWN.

MAY

2	9	16	23	30
3	10	17	24	31
4	11	18	25	
5	12	19	26	
6	13	20	27	
7	14	21	28	
1 8	15	22	29	

COMPETITION

Just got back in from the local comp at the skatepark near my house. I'm stoked! The judges decided to have a jam format for the comp. In a jam all the skaters ride together and the judges pick out a few skaters who impress them. The session was amazing. The best thing of all is that the guy who owns the local skate shop asked me if I'd like to ride for their team, too!

There were a few professional skaters at the contest. Andy Scott turned up and destroyed everything! This noseblunt on the back rail of the quarterpipe was so smooth. I can't believe he did it.

NOTE:
Sponsorship only means that a company or shop gives you free boards, so that you can go out and get photos riding their equipment in magazines or skate videos. You don't actually get paid unless you're a professional skater with your own signature boards.

22

Competitions are an excuse for loads of skaters to get together and session. Everyone pushes everyone else and some crazy tricks get landed.

I did a frontside flip and a 360 flip over the hip this guy is skating. I'd never landed the 360 flip before, but the atmosphere of the session really pushed me.

23

JUNE

	6	13	20	27
	7	14	21	28
1	8	15	22	29
2	9	16	23	30
3	10	17	24
4	11	18	25
5	12	19	26

SPONSORSHIP

Things have moved fast since I got on the skate-shop team. I've entered a few other competitions around our area, and I went out and shot photos with a photographer from a magazine for the first time yesterday. That was very strange. I had to say which trick I wanted to do at which spot first. Then when we got there I had to perform on cue. It was okay though, once I'd calmed down a little bit.

My dad took a photo of someone videoing me. Weird!

HISTORY — Sponsorship for skateboarders started in the 1970s. One of the most famous teams from that era was the Zephyr team. That was a skate-shop team too — with old-school legends like Tony Alva and Jay Adams riding for it. I feel privileged to be following in their footsteps.

Now I'm a nearly pro rider, I'm trying to keep fitter. I go running twice a week and swimming once, and I'm even trying to eat healthy fresh fruit instead of chocolate (sometimes!).

24

I'm always scared of hitting the camera, but they're pretty good at getting out of the way!

SKATE GODS

As I've got more and more involved in skateboarding I've started trying to find out a little bit more about some of the most progressive skaters over the ages. I've been researching some of the older skaters on the internet too, along with some of the modern skaters who inspire me. I've even made a scrapbook with some of my favourite skaters in it.

Duane Peters, one of the most talented skaters ever, skating a backyard swimming pool.

Duane Peters
Skates for: Red Cross Skateboards; used to skate for Santa Cruz, the world's oldest skateboard company.
Famous as: The original punk-rock skater, whose fearless, do-or-die attitude changed skateboarding forever.
Speciality: Invented many of the tricks we take for granted today, for example the rock and roll. One of the few 70s stars who still appears in skate mags today.

Tony Trujillo
From: California, USA
Skates for: 'Anti Hero'
Famous as: Oozes style; recently won the 'Skater of the Year' award in *Thrasher* magazine.
Speciality: Skates everything from stairs to huge bowls really fast, really smooth.

Paul Rodriguez
From: California, USA
Skates for: US board company 'Girl'
Famous as: Teenaged skater who got really good, really quickly. His skating is technical, smooth and powerful.
Speciality: Skates difficult ledge tricks on big obstacles.

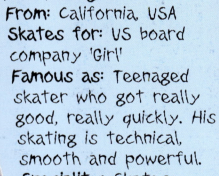

Paul Rodriguez, frontside noseslide on a real handrail.

27

JULY

	4	11	18	25
	5	12	19	26
	6	13	20	27
	7	14	21	28
1	8	15	22	29
2	9	16	23	30
3	10	(17)	24	31

TAILSLIDES — I REALLY LIKE THIS ONE BECAUSE YOU CAN TAILSLIDE ANYTHING FROM A POOL TO A LEDGE. IT'S A REALLY VERSATILE TRICK.

APPROACH THE LEDGE OR COPING WITH YOUR FEET IN OLLIE POSITION AT A MODERATE SPEED.

OLLIE AND TURN THROUGH 90 DEGREES SO THAT YOU WILL LAND ON THE TAIL.

ADVANCED SKATING

I've been pushing myself really hard and I've learned a load of new tricks. I picked some of the things that my favourite skaters do and just studied them over and over again until I worked out how to do it. If I want to take my skating further I need to be constantly improving my skating and riding bigger and faster obstacles.

I want to learn these! Backside tailslides are my favourite trick but they're so hard. I'm going to learn, though.

28

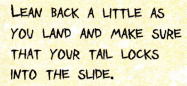

LEAN BACK A LITTLE AS YOU LAND AND MAKE SURE THAT YOUR TAIL LOCKS INTO THE SLIDE.

SLIDE FOR AS LONG AS POSSIBLE AND THEN TURN YOUR SHOULDERS TO UNLOCK YOURSELF.

RIDE AWAY FORWARDS.

FRONTSIDE AIRS:

Tony Alva invented this trick in the late 1970s. The technique is a little different these days, but it's basically the same trick. It's easiest to do this on a big transition because having plenty of speed helps.

1 Ride up the transition.

2 As you get to the top, ollie frontside and prepare to grab with your back hand.

3 Grab the board as you peak and point your front foot forwards.

4 As you fall back towards the ramp release your grab.

5 Land back into the transition on all four wheels and ride away.

SKATEBOARD WORDS

360 flip
A variation of the more basic kickflip. The board rotates through 360 degrees while flipping on its axis.

Backside
This is a term that came from surfing and is used to describe the direction of a trick. Imagine yourself riding up a mini-ramp transition: if your back is facing the top as you turn, you are moving in a backside direction.

Beast
A term used to describe an impressive trick or skater's style, especially where speed and style are involved.

Blindside
A term used to describe any aerial trick where the skater is travelling backwards without being able to see the point of landing.

Durometer
A measurement of skateboard wheel hardness. Most modern wheels fall between 95 and 100a on the durometer.

Frontside
This is the opposite of backside. Visualize yourself on a ramp: if you are facing the top as you turn then you are moving in a frontside direction.

Grind
A trick where the trucks slide along an obstacle.

Hardness (wheels)
Harder wheels (around 100a) allow the skater to slide from one direction to the other. The harder the wheel the more it will slide. Softer wheels are faster and have more grip, and are used by downhill and slalom skaters.

Hip
A skate obstacle where two banks or ramps meet, making an L-shaped hip. Most skateparks have hips of some variety.

Local
A term used to describe a skater who regularly rides a local spot or skatepark.

Nollie
A switch-stance, fakie ollie invented by Natas Kaupas in the late 1980s; an ollie off the nose of your board while travelling forwards.

Noseblunt
Balancing on the coping of a ramp on your front wheels, with your nose pointing down into the transition.

Nosebone
To contort the board and body whilst grabbing in the air for extra style points. Also known as 'tweaking', 'boning' or 'torque'.

Quarterpipe
A classic skate obstacle, which comes in many different shapes and sizes. A quarterpipe is one half of a half pipe.

Stinking

A derogatory term used to describe a trick done without style, speed or flow.

Stoked

A state of excitement produced by a good skate session. Also known as 'amped' and 'buzzing'.

Varial flip

Any flip variation where the board rotates through 180 degrees whilst flipping.

INTERNET LINKS

www.sidewalkmag.com

The site of Europe's biggest English-language magazine, with links to other sites, hundreds of video clips, message board and news.

www.skateboardermag.com

Useful site from the best skate mag out of the States, packed with information, reviews and more.

www.thrashermagazine.com

Long-established site of US skate magazine Thrasher, with competitions, news, trick tips and more.

www.skateboarding.com

Another general-purpose skating site, with news, feature articles, photos and more.

www.skateboardeurope.com

A useful European site, with information about contests and events from all over Europe.

MAGAZINES

I read a lot of skateboard magazines (mainly UK and US ones) to keep up to date on who's doing what trick-wise and to find out information on coming events, competitions, tours and what not. My favourite magazines are Sidewalk (UK magazine) and Thrasher and Skateboarder magazines from the States.

VIDEOS

I also watch a lot of skateboard videos as they often have footage of top riders and new parks. My favourites are 411 video magazine and the Transworld videos as far as the US goes and Puzzle or Blueprint videos in Europe.

DISCLAIMER
All the Internet addresses (URLs) Kitch has given in this book were valid at the time of going to press. However, due to the dynamic nature of the Internet, some addresses may have changed, or sites may have changed or ceased to exist since publication. While the author and Publisher regret any inconvenience this may cause readers, no responsibility for any such changes can be accepted by either the author or the Publisher.

INDEX